gravest danger – to him and, as it turned out, to so many others – might come from within."

What is it about us human beings that, though we are so wonderfully made, incredibly intelligent and creative, we find ourselves living in a way that in our better moments appals us? We know the symptoms, but what is really wrong with us as people?

Jesus answered that question when He said, "What comes out of you is what defiles you. For from within, out of your hearts, come evil thoughts, sexual immorality, theft, murder, adultery, greed, malice, deceit, lewdness, envy, slander, arrogance and folly. All these evils come from inside and defile you." [2]

## Take a closer look

The claims of Christianity are of such significance that it behoves us all to take a closer look at Jesus, who He is and what He has done.

We were created an
enjoy the life God h
very personal way.
the first human bein
and brought into cr
havoc in our lives a

GW00706143

James, wrote in the Bible, 'What is causing the quarrels and fights among you? Isn't it the whole army of evil desires at war within you?'[3] Our sin – the breaking of God's commandments – is serious. It cuts us off from God, will keep us out of heaven, and would condemn us to hell.

There is something strangely fascinating about the scandals in the lives of others. The fact that some celebrity is being exposed brings a wry smile to us, possibly because we are well aware that we have been guilty of the same misdemeanours, but no one would be interested in the details of our lives. It is striking that the Bible's diagnosis is that the greatest problem we face is that all of us have sinned against God.

There is another major problem that confronts us. It is a result of our having sinned against God. Like cut flowers, which bring so much pleasure for a while, but soon wither and die, we too will one day die. Death is an unwelcome intruder

3    James 4:1

into our lives and plans. The best of doctors, fitness programmes and vitamins all fail when the 'Grim Reaper' approaches. Something inside us cries out that there must be an answer, otherwise life is meaningless. David Mellor was a Cabinet Minister and is now a radio presenter. Recently at the Royal Society of Portrait Painters he said what many must feel, "Everything I have done in life has been redundant. My life has been one exercise in futility." Without God in a person's life, that is the logical conclusion.

If that was the sum total of the Christian message, we would have little reason to rejoice, and yet Christians are joyful people. It is not that they, like the ostrich, have buried their heads in the sand, but rather have faced the issue and found that God has the answer to their dilemma.

## The hiding place

I love the story of the little girl who answered the phone only to hear the question,

> *"Is your father there?"*

> *"Yes!" the little girl whispered.*

> *"Then could I speak to him, please?"*

> *"No! He's very busy," the girl replied in a low whisper.*

*"Well, is your mother there?"*

*"Yes! But she is very busy too."*

*"Is anybody else there?" the man asked again.*

*Still whispering, the girl answered, "Yes, the police are here."*

*"Then could I speak with a police officer please?"*

*"No! They're very busy as well."*

*"Is anybody else there?" the man asked, becoming exasperated.*

*"Yes, the fire-brigade are here?" the girl said, still whispering, "But they are busy too."*

*"What is going on, with so many people there and everybody is busy?"*

*Innocently but quietly she answered, "They're all looking for me!"*

Hiding is a childish adventure, in which we have all have been involved. It can be quite exciting. But to be on the run from our Maker and God is a different matter altogether. The stark fact is that we have not only run from God, but rebelled against Him with our wrong thoughts, words and deeds. Our sins and evil deeds have separated us from the altogether good God.

It is strangely perverse that though God has given us our lives, we want to turn from Him. God has revealed to us who He is and what He is like. He is a spirit; we cannot touch or see Him. God knows all things and can do everything. He is everywhere and so sees us running from Him! He is so absolutely pure, just, loving, reliable and unchanging.

So great is His compassion towards us that the message of the Bible is that He has come looking for us! There is only one God, who is Father, Son and Holy Spirit. He is a personal and relational God. We have become strange creatures when we prefer our dark ways to God's light and life and love! God is eternal, with no beginning or end. And the Father sent the Son to be the Saviour of the world. Having gone our own way Jesus came to bring us back into a relationship with God Himself.

Jesus said of His mission, "I ... have come to seek and save those that are lost,"[4] and "For even I, the Son of Man, came here not to be served but to serve others, and to give my life a ransom for many."[5]

The idea of a ransom being paid to redeem individuals is not foreign to our thinking. Once in a while we hear of a demand for a ransom. Frank Sinatra Jnr, Eric Peugeot (son of the car manufacturer), and John Paul Getty III were each redeemed with millions of pounds after having been kidnapped as children.

4    Luke 19:10
5    Mark 10:45

## Husband buys back his wife!

Hosea lived 2,700 years ago. He was a well-known preacher in his community. When he announced he was to marry, you can imagine that it was the talk of the town. God had guided Him to marry a woman called Gomer. Every detail of their lives would have been scrutinised. In time, they had a son and daughter, but then disaster struck, which would have been hard for the ordinary onlooker to believe. Gomer walked out on Hosea to become a prostitute. It was totally humiliating to Hosea. In time God instructed Hosea to go, find and then buy back his wife. Imagine some of the places he had to search to locate her … and he was a prophet! He eventually found his wife in the market place, about to be auctioned off as a slave. Hosea stood in the crowd and with silver and barley out-bid everyone else. He redeemed his wife. She was his by right, and he was hers – they were married; but now she was doubly his. She had been redeemed at a great price.

In the heartache of the story of Hosea is an illustration of a great truth. Like Gomer, the nation of Israel, as well as us today, had sold themselves to do wrong: to live with little thought of God. Hosea did what God was eventually going to do, that is to buy back what was rightfully His. For Hosea the price was great; for God the price to redeem us was greater still.

The Bible is God's written message to humanity. It reveals Him to us. It describes the marvellous moment in history when God took on Himself a human body and made His dwelling among us. Like two musical keys on a piano being played at the same moment and blending into one chord, so the nature of God and man perfectly blended in the person of Jesus Christ. He was fully God and fully human. He was God, taking the initiative in coming to reach, rescue and redeem us.

Jesus came to buy and bring us back to God, but euros, pounds or dollars could never be a sufficient a price for that. The price that Jesus paid was His own blood.

Peter, the disciple of Jesus, wrote to Christians in different parts of the world saying, ' You were not redeemed with corruptible things, like silver or gold, from your aimless conduct received by tradition from your fathers, but with the precious blood of Christ …'[6]

Paul, who wrote many of the books in the New Testament part of the Bible, said, '… in (Jesus) we have redemption through His blood, the forgiveness of sins, according to the riches of His grace which He made to abound toward us …'[7]

## The ransom paid

Religions of the world tell us to try our best and work our way to God. But are we really to believe that any human being could be good enough to impress God, who is unapproachably pure? The Bible tells us that God is too great and holy for small, sinful humans to reach. Yet, God, in His immense love, has come for us.

He has not dismissed us, but neither has He overlooked the guilt of our lives. In Jesus, God has provided a costly ransom to deal with our sin and to buy us back into the relationship with Him for which we were created. All the headline-hitting crimes of the world, as well as the hidden sins of the ordinary millions of men and women who simply go about their lives unnoticed by others, were all laid on Jesus when He was crucified at Calvary. He, the eternal One,

6   1 Peter 1:18 - 19
7   Ephesians 1:7 & 8

carried the can for our sin. He died, was buried in a cave, and three days later rose again.

Through the death and resurrection of Jesus we can have forgiveness, freedom and a forever-relationship with God. Jesus will bring us to know God, as we trust Him to be our Lord and Saviour.

This totally transforms our attitude to everything that life presents to us. The Holy Spirit of God comes to actually live within the lives of those who trust Jesus. The 18th century preacher, John Wesley, said of fellow Christians, "Best of all God is with us." That is what Jesus promised. He is there as a friend through the good and tough times of life. The Bible says, 'For (God) Himself has said, "I will never leave you nor forsake you." So we may boldly say: "The Lord is my helper; I will not fear. What can man do to me?"'[8]

## A story from the West ... and from the East

Uncle Tom's Cabin was the best selling novel of the 19th century. Written by Harriet Beecher Stowe, it tells the story of a long-suffering black slave who is sold by his owner in Kentucky, to pay off his debts. Eventually Tom is sold again to a cruel cotton plantation owner, who one day beats him to within an inch of death. Belatedly, the son of

---

8   Hebrews 13:5 & 6

UNCLE TOM'S CABIN

TOPSY.

Tom's first master arrives to redeem Tom. He finds him lying in a shed and pleads saying, "You shan't die! You mustn't die, nor think of it. I've come to buy you and take you home."

Tom's reply is potent: 'O Mas'r George, ye're too late. The Lord's bought me, and is going to take me home – and I long to go. Heaven is better than Kintuck."

But that is fiction. In real life, a man named Job lived centuries ago in the East. He was devout and well respected in his community, until his world collapsed around him. Within days, each of his children died in freak incidents, his business collapsed and his body was tortured with numerous illnesses. Neither he, nor those who tried to comfort him, understood what was happening. And yet in that dire suffering he trusted in God. He said, "I know that my Redeemer lives, and that in the end He will stand upon the earth. After my skin has been destroyed, yet in my flesh I will see God; I myself will see Him with my own eyes – I, not another."[9]

Job lived long before Jesus, but just as we look back to Christ, Job looked forward to the time when Jesus would come. He also had a confidence that one day God would rule over all creation.

No one relishes the idea of suffering or death! Christians, though, have a confidence that Jesus their Redeemer will be with them throughout life, through death, and into eternity. It is not that they are good enough for God and heaven – nobody is - but rather that all which would condemn them has been forgiven. Heaven is not a reward; it is a gift. The Bible says, 'For the wages of sin is death, but the gift of God is eternal life in Christ Jesus our Lord.'[10] Christians are people who have been made right with God when they turned from their sin, and trusted Jesus to be their Redeemer - their Lord, Saviour and Friend. They have found that Jesus is the answer to the problems of sin, death and meaninglessness.

Would you be willing to trust Jesus in this way? Are you longing that Jesus, the Redeemer, would now bring you to know God? Are you wanting to put your trust in Jesus and receive Him as Lord of your life?

---

9    Job 19:25 - 27
10    Romans 6:23

## I took a closer look

I was converted to Christ when I was fifteen years of age. I was on holiday in the Middle East where a relative, who worked as a Christian minister, explained the good news of Jesus to me. He asked me if I had ever trusted Jesus Christ in this way. Clearly I hadn't, but I knew that I wanted to. He explained to me that following Jesus can be tough, but I simply felt that if Jesus had died for me, then I must trust Him.

That very day, sitting on a log on the mountains of the Lebanon, I prayed asking Jesus to become my Lord and Saviour, as I committed my life to Him. I have never regretted that moment. There was no flash in the sky, but neither was it a flash in the pan. The greatest joy of my life has been to live it with Christ as my Redeemer. I encourage you too to trust Him in this way.

Many people have found that praying words like these have been helpful, as they have committed their lives to Jesus:

Dear God, thank you that you know everything there is to know about me. I am sorry for all my sin, and with your help I want to turn from it. Thank you that Jesus came to earth, to die for my sin. Thank you that He rose again from the dead and is alive. Please forgive me. By your Holy Spirit come to live in my life,